Action Art

Using colour

Isabel Thomas

www.raintreepublishers.co.uk

Visit our website to find out more information about **Raintree** books.

To order:

 Phone 44 (0) 1865 888112

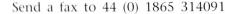 Send a fax to 44 (0) 1865 314091

 Visit the Raintree Bookshop at **www.raintreepublishers.co.uk** to browse our catalogue and order online.

First published in Great Britain by Raintree, Halley Court, Jordan Hill, Oxford OX2 8EJ, part of Harcourt Education.
Raintree is a registered trademark of Harcourt Education Ltd.

Editorial: Melanie Copland, Kate Buckingham and Lucy Beevor
Design: Jo Malivoire and AMR
Picture Research: Mica Brancic
Production: Duncan Gilbert
Originated by Modern Age
Printed and bound in China by South China Printing Company

ISBN 1 844 21240 8 (hardback)
09 08 07 06 05
10 9 8 7 6 5 4 3 2 1

British Library Cataloguing in Publication Data
Thomas, Isabel
Using colour – (Action Art)
752
A full catalogue record for this book is available from the British Library.

Acknowledgements
Alamy p. 5; Corbis pp. 4, 14; Harcourt Education p. 10 (Trevor Clifford) pp. 6, 7, 8, 9, 11, 12, 13, 15, 16, 17, 18, 19, 20, 21, 22, 23, 24 (Tudor Photography)

Cover photograph of hand painting reproduced with permission of Corbis

Every effort has been made to contact copyright holders of any material reproduced in this book. Any omissions will be rectified in subsequent printings if notice is given to the publishers.

The paper used to print this book comes from sustainable resources.

Disclaimer
All the Internet addresses (URLs) given in this book were valid at the time of going to press. However, due to the dynamic nature of the Internet, some addresses may have changed, or sites may have changed or ceased to exist since publication. While the author and publishers regret any inconvenience this may cause readers, no responsibility for any such changes can be accepted by either the author or the publishers.

Some words are shown in bold, **like this**. You can find them in the glossary on page 23.

Contents

What is art?

Art is something you make when you are being **creative**.

People like to look at art.

A person who makes art is called an artist.

You can be an artist too!

What kinds of art are there?

There are many different kinds of art.

You can draw and paint pictures.

sculpture

Try making sculptures and collage too.

You can use colour in all your art.

What are primary colours?

Red, yellow, and blue are called **primary colours**.

We mix them together to make other colours.

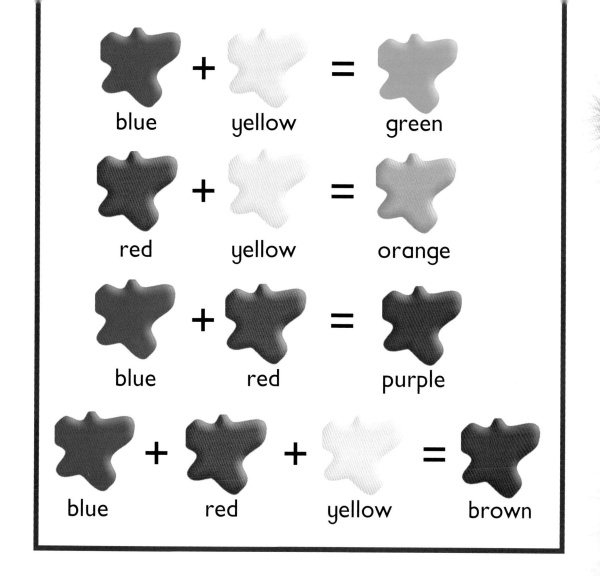

blue + yellow = green

red + yellow = orange

blue + red = purple

blue + red + yellow = brown

Try mixing paints to make these new colours.

You can use a brush or your fingers!

How can I make colours lighter or darker?

There are light and dark **shades** of every colour.

Look at the different shades of blue in this picture.

black

blue

white

Make a colour darker by adding black paint.

Add white paint to make a colour lighter.

What can I use for colouring?

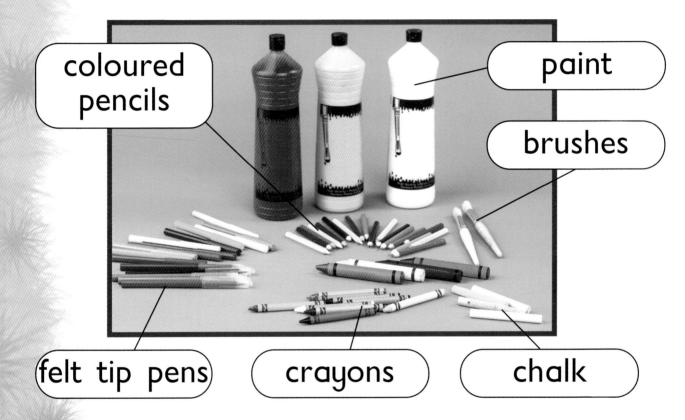

coloured pencils

paint

brushes

felt tip pens

crayons

chalk

Look at all the **tools** that you can use for colouring.

You can use colourful paper and objects to make art, too.

You can make a colourful collage.

How can I use colour?

You can use colour to make art look interesting.

Use paints to colour your sculptures.

Colour in your drawings carefully.

Try to keep the colour inside
the lines.

How can I make a pattern?

You can use lots of colours to make a **pattern**.

Try using patterns to **decorate** things.

Potato printing is a fun way to make patterns.

Print a border for your art.

How do colours make me feel?

Colours can make us feel different things.

Bright colours make you feel happy.

What colours would you use to paint a bright and sunny day?

Let's use colour!

Let's use colour to make a fish!

1. Use a wax crayon to draw the shape of a big fish.

2. Fill in the shape using lots of different coloured crayons. You can draw green seaweed, too.

20

3. Now paint over your drawing with watery blue paint.

4. You have made a picture of a fish in the sea!

Quiz

Can you remember which colours you need to add to make these colours?

green = blue + ?

brown = yellow + red + ?

orange = yellow + ?

purple = red + ?

Look for the answers on page 24.

Glossary

 **creative** making something using your own ideas and how you feel inside

 **decorate** add colours and patterns to make something look nice

 **pattern** the same shapes and colours used over and over again

 **primary colours** red, blue, and yellow are called primary colours

 **shades** different kinds of one colour. Light blue and dark blue are different shades of blue.

 **tools** the things you use for colouring in, like pencils and crayons

Index

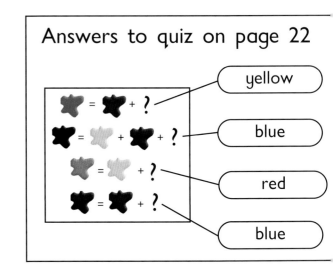

Answers to quiz on page 22

yellow

blue

red

blue